ANCIENT CIVILIZATIONS
A DAY IN THE INCA EMPIRE

by Janie Havemeyer
illustrated by Cesar Samaniego

Tools for Parents & Teachers

Grasshopper Books enhance imagination and introduce the earliest readers to fun storylines and illustrations. The easy-to-read text supports early reading experiences with repetitive sentence patterns and sight words.

Before Reading
- Discuss the cover illustration. What do readers see?
- Look at the glossary together. Discuss the words.

Read the Book
- Read the book to the child, or have them read independently.
- "Walk" through the book and look at the illustrations. When and where does the story take place? What is happening in the story?

After Reading
- Prompt the child to think more. Ask: What was life like in the Inca Empire? What more would you like to learn about this time period?

Grasshopper Books are published by Jump!
5357 Penn Avenue South
Minneapolis, MN 55419
www.jumplibrary.com

Copyright © 2025 Jump! International copyright reserved in all countries. No part of this book may be reproduced in any form without written permission from the publisher.

Library of Congress Cataloging-in-Publication Data

Names: Havemeyer, Janie, author.
Samaniego, César, 1975- illustrator.
Title: A day in the Inca Empire / by Janie Havemeyer; illustrated by Cesar Samaniego.
Description: Minneapolis, MN: Jump!, Inc., [2025]
Series: Ancient civilizations | Includes index.
Audience: Ages 7-10
Identifiers: LCCN 2024030477 (print)
LCCN 2024030478 (ebook)
ISBN 9798892134897 (hardcover)
ISBN 9798892134903 (paperback)
ISBN 9798892134910 (ebook)
Subjects: LCSH: Incas–Social life and customs–Juvenile literature. | Peru–Civilization–Juvenile literature. Machu Picchu Site (Peru)–Juvenile literature.
Classification: LCC F3429 .H35 2025 (print)
LCC F3429 (ebook)
DDC 985/.019–dc23/eng/20240718
LC record available at https://lccn.loc.gov/2024030477
LC ebook record available at https://lccn.loc.gov/2024030478

Editor: Alyssa Sorenson
Direction and Layout: Anna Peterson
Illustrator: Cesar Samaniego
Content Consultant: Christopher Heaney, PhD, Associate Professor of Latin American History, The Pennsylvania State University

Printed in the United States of America at Corporate Graphics in North Mankato, Minnesota.

Table of Contents

A Large Empire	4
Inca Empire Timeline	22
Map of the Inca Empire	23
To Learn More	23
Glossary	24
Index	24

A Large Empire

It is summer in the year 1470. The Andes Mountains surround Cuzco in South America. This city is the **capital** of the Inca **Empire**.

A **herder** wakes up early. He straps packs onto his llamas. He fills them with alpaca wool. He will bring it to the city to trade. People will use the wool to make clothing.

A runner leaves the city. He races over a long rope bridge. He carries a **quipu** from the **emperor**. It has a message. He will pass it to other runners on the road. They will deliver it to Machu Picchu. This is another city in the large empire. It is 50 miles (80 kilometers) away.

In Cuzco, a **noble** family has breakfast. They eat corn bread on silver plates.

Afterward, the father and son join the emperor in the forest. They hunt deer with slingshots.

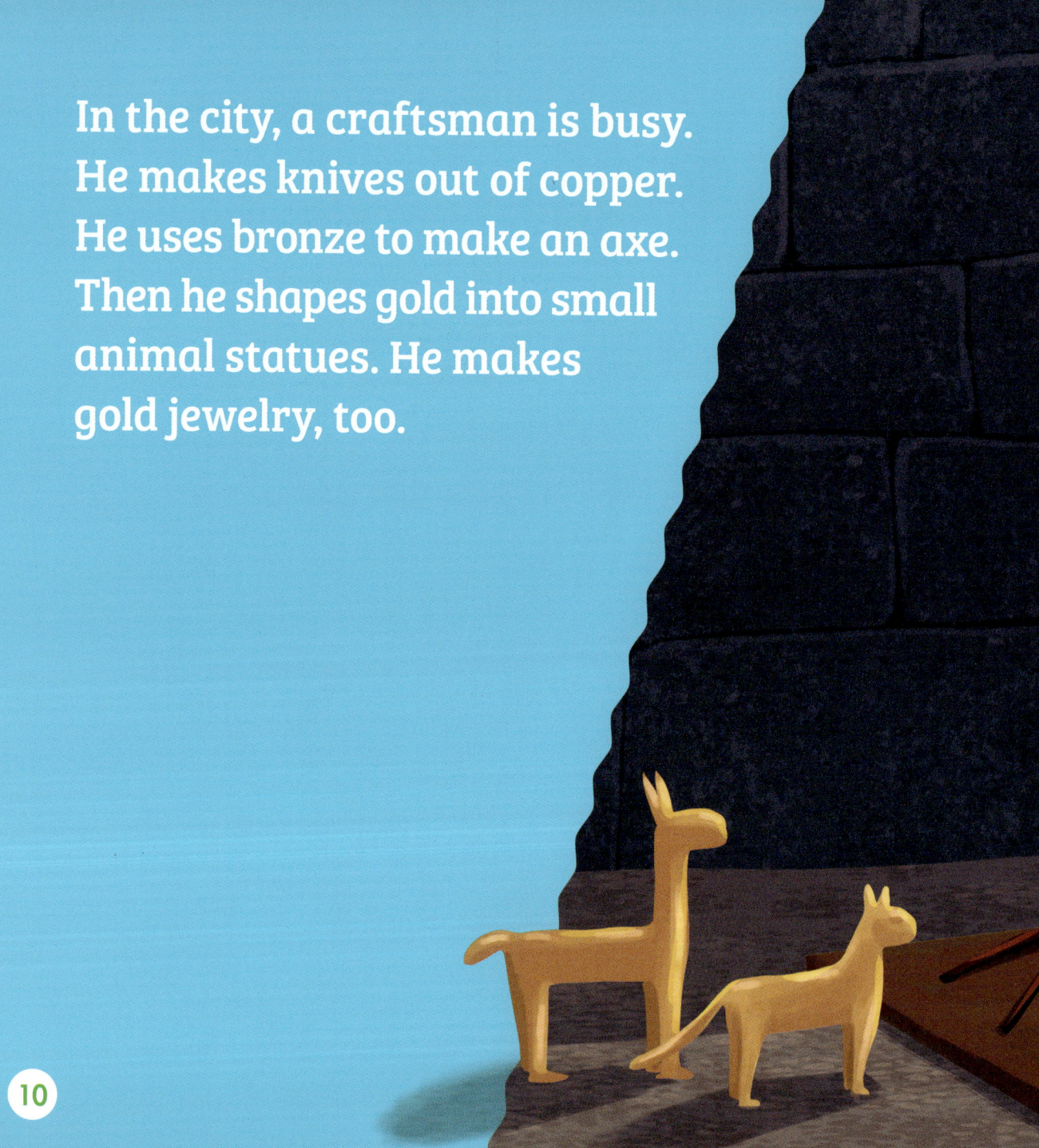

In the city, a craftsman is busy. He makes knives out of copper. He uses bronze to make an axe. Then he shapes gold into small animal statues. He makes gold jewelry, too.

In the afternoon, a woman cooks over a fire. She cares for her baby.

Her daughter collects firewood. Her son fixes a net to catch birds. The family will eat the birds he catches. They will trade the bright bird feathers.

Outside the city, workers dig into the side of a mountain. They are making flat areas. Farmers will plant corn and potatoes here in fall. These plants feed the people of the Inca Empire.

A large crowd gathers in the city. They celebrate the Festival of the Sun. It honors Inti, the Sun **god**. The emperor sits on top of a platform. Musicians beat drums. Others blow panpipes.

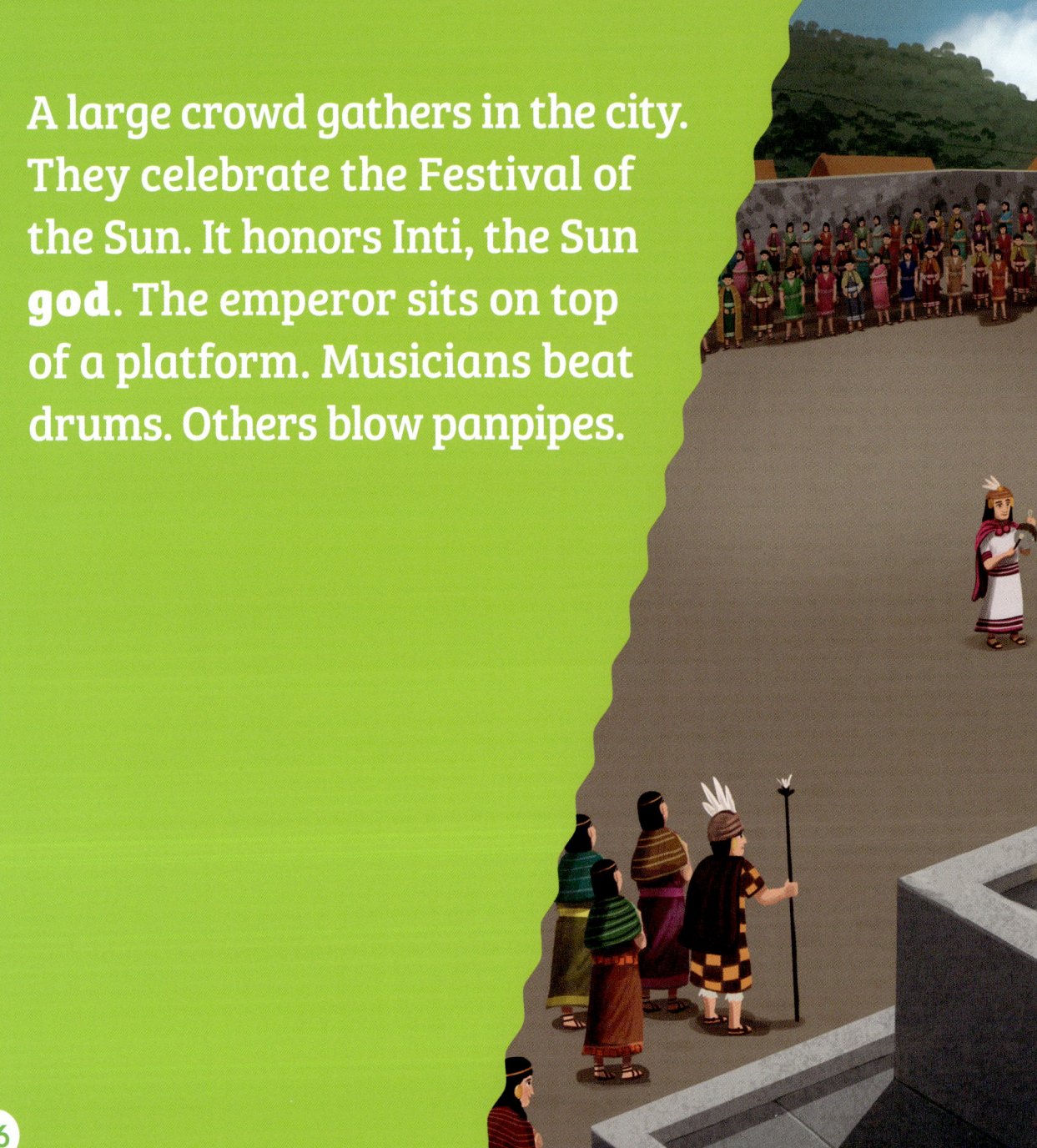

People place **royal** mummies on stools. They believe the mummies link them to important **ancestors**, like Inti. People treat the mummies as if they are still alive. They bring them gifts. Men sing about their victories. Dancers perform.

A runner reaches Machu Picchu. He delivers the emperor's message. The emperor will visit Machu Picchu soon. He wants everything to be ready for him.

The runner wraps himself in a blanket made of llama wool. He falls asleep under the bright stars that shine on the Inca Empire.

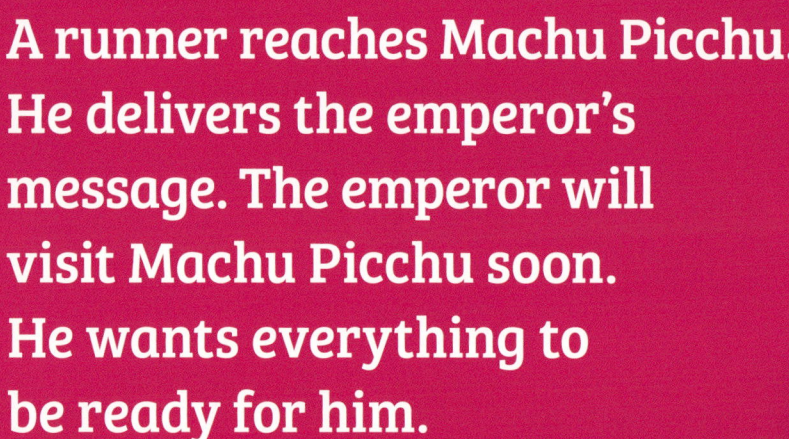

Inca Empire Timeline

What are some important events in the Inca Empire's history? Take a look!

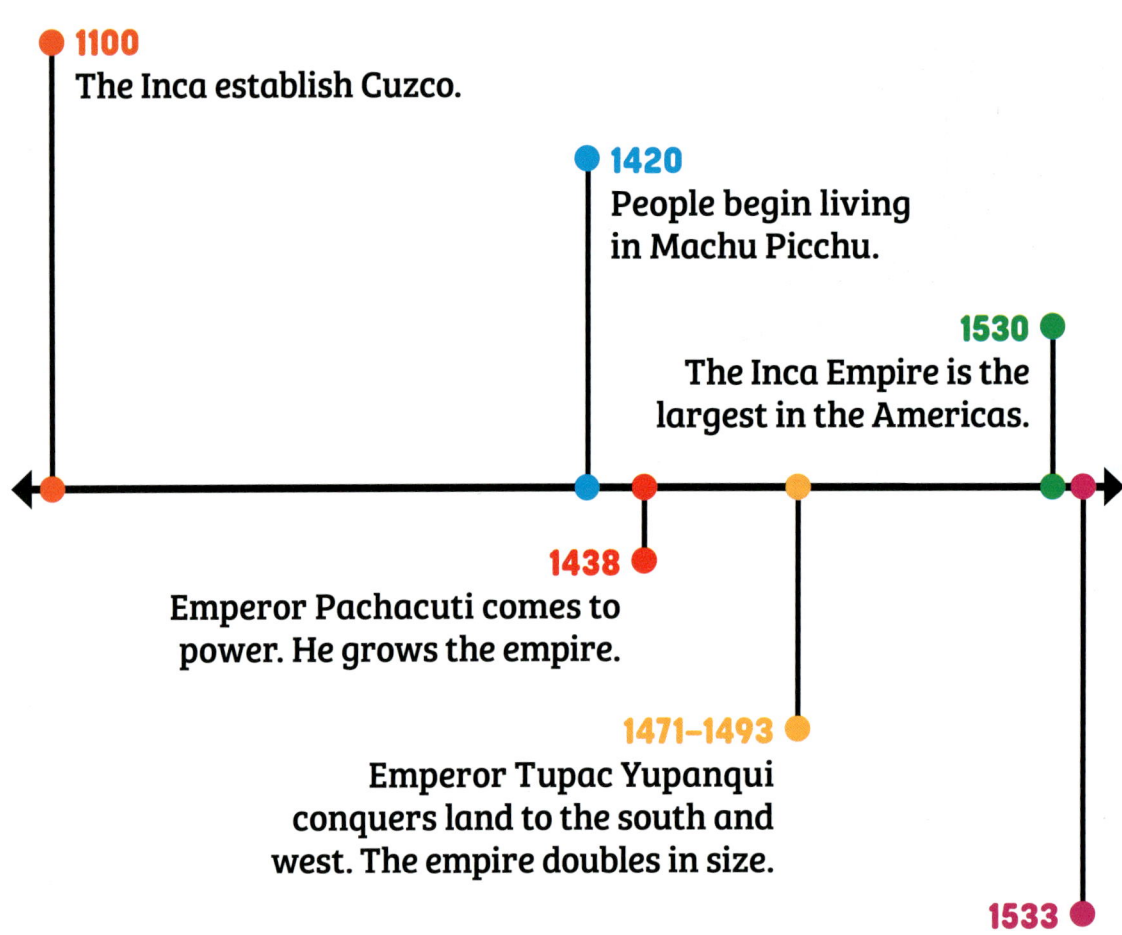

- **1100** — The Inca establish Cuzco.
- **1420** — People begin living in Machu Picchu.
- **1438** — Emperor Pachacuti comes to power. He grows the empire.
- **1471–1493** — Emperor Tupac Yupanqui conquers land to the south and west. The empire doubles in size.
- **1530** — The Inca Empire is the largest in the Americas.
- **1533** — The Spanish kill Emperor Atahualpa. The Inca Empire collapses.

Map of the Inca Empire

Take a look at the Inca Empire in 1470.

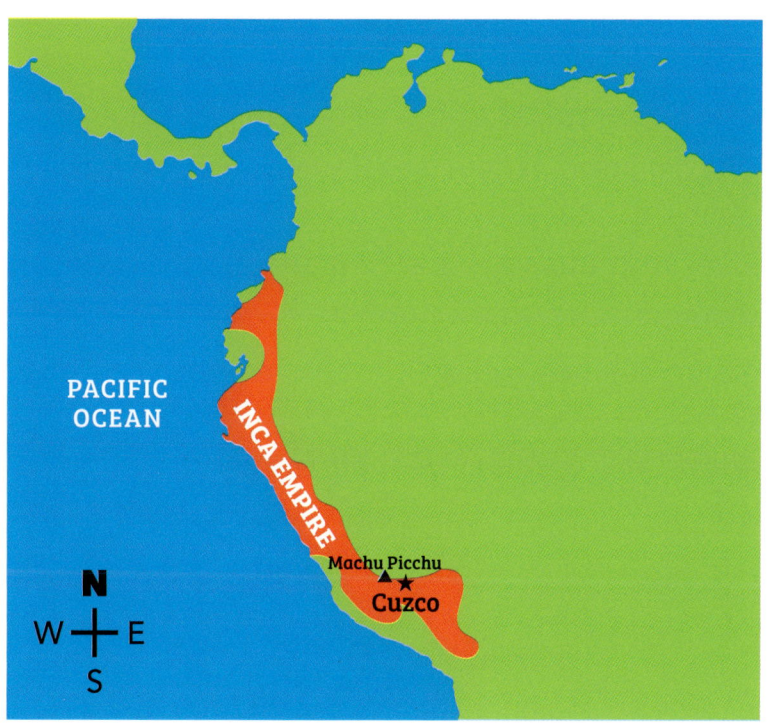

To Learn More

Finding more information is as easy as 1, 2, 3.
1. Go to www.factsurfer.com
2. Enter "**IncaEmpire**" into the search box.
3. Choose your book to see a list of websites.

Glossary

ancestors: Members of one's family who lived long ago.

capital: The city in a country where the government is based.

emperor: A male ruler of an empire.

empire: A group of countries or states that have the same ruler.

god: A being that is worshipped and believed to have special powers over nature and life.

herder: Someone who moves animals together in a group.

noble: Of high social position.

quipu: A device with knots on colored strings that have been carefully arranged into a message.

royal: Relating to an emperor or a member of their family.

Index

Andes Mountains 4

craftsman 10

Cuzco 4, 8

emperor 6, 9, 16, 20

farmers 14

Festival of the Sun 16

herder 5

Inti 16, 18

llamas 5, 20

Machu Picchu 6, 20

mummies 18

runner 6, 20